Contents

The fishes shown below are representatives of the principal groups found in Britain and Europe. Under each illustration is a reference to the pages on which that group is described and illustrated, and a symbol or symbols to indicate whether the group is found in fresh water, salt water or both: O fresh water, ● salt water.

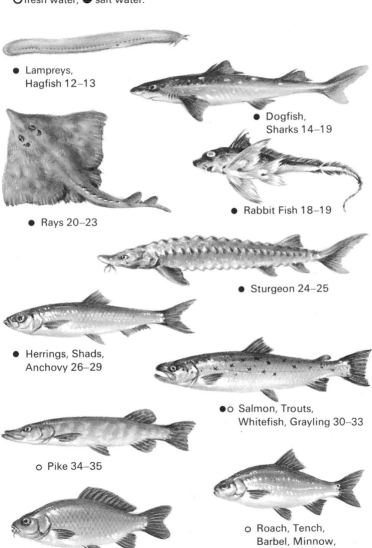

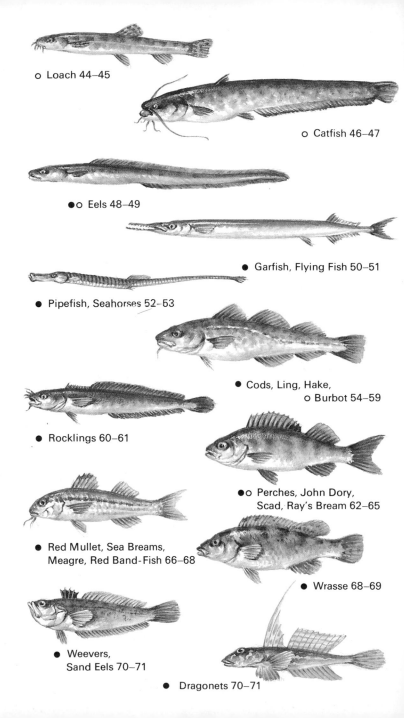

- Mackerel, Tunnies, Swordfish 72–75

- Gobies 76–77

- Blennies 78–79

- Butterfish 78–79

- Grey Mullets, Sand-Smelts 80–81

- Gurnards, Redfish 82–83

●o Bullheads 84–85

- Sea Snails, Lumpsucker 84–85

●o Sticklebacks 86–87

- Flatfish 88–91

- Clingfish 93

- Angler Fish 92

Introduction

WHAT IS A FISH? Fish are aquatic vertebrates which breathe by means of gills. Other aquatic animals are often loosely described as fish but they can be easily distinguished by the basic structure of their bodies. For example shellfish are not true fish because they do not have a backbone while whales and porpoises, although vertebrates and living permanently in water, are mammals and breathe through lungs.

KINDS OF FISH Fishes can be divided into three major types: bony, cartilaginous and jawless. Bony fishes, such as Herring, Salmon, Carp and Perch, are the most numerous; they are characterized by a skeleton containing bone and a gill-cover over the gill slits on each side of the head. All the bony fishes in this book (apart from Sturgeon) are 'teleosts' with a tail fin which appears symmetrical above and below the midline of the body, and the body usually covered with tiny flat bones called scales. Cartilaginous fishes include sharks, dogfish, skates and rays; they tend to be larger in size, their skeletons are composed of cartilage, not bone, and males have 'claspers' on the pelvic fins for mating. Other characteristics include a skin with numerous small teeth-like projections which form the series of teeth over the jaws and which are sometimes enlarged as thorns and spines on the body surface; they also have separate gill slits (usually five, with a small anterior pore, the spiracle) on the side, or undersurface of the head, no gill cover (except in Rabbit Fish), and usually a prominent snout. Jawless fishes are relicts from the past which have persisted as the parasitic and scavenging lampreys and Hagfish; they do not have true jaws, lack bone in the skeleton, have no paired fins and their horny teeth are quite unlike those of other fish; the gill openings are individual pores (seven on each side in European lampreys) or a single pair in the Hagfish.

BODY AND FINS Fish are streamlined to minimize energy spent on swimming and possess fins which work in various ways as hydrofoils. The dorsal, anal and caudal fins are referred to as the 'median' fins while the pectoral and pelvic (ventral) fins are 'paired'. Bony fishes have membranous fins supported by bony rays; in cartilaginous fishes the rays are horny and the fins much less flexible. Fishes swim by using the blocks of muscle on each side of the supple backbone to produce wave-like movements of the rear body and caudal fin which propel the fish forwards. The other fins act as stabilizers against rolling, yawing and pitching of the moving body and also act as brakes. The shape and positioning of the fins varies according to the habits and habitat of the species. For example, oceanic sharks and tunnies have crescent-shaped caudal fins more suited for fast swimming. Perch have deeper bodies, higher-sited pectoral fins and pelvic fins shifted forward to increase manoevrability. Bottom-living fish are modified in many different ways for life on the sea-bed. In gobies, sea-snails and clingfish, the pelvic fins are fused into a ventral sucker for temporary anchorage to the sea-bed; Eels are elongate to enable them to

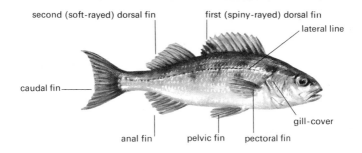

second (soft-rayed) dorsal fin first (spiny-rayed) dorsal fin
lateral line
caudal fin
gill-cover
anal fin pelvic fin pectoral fin

wriggle under stones; skates and rays, which lie belly-down on the bottom, are flattened downwards while the Plaice and Sole which swim on the right or left side are compressed sideways. Skates move by wavy rippling of the edges of the broad pectoral 'wings', flatfish by similar use of the dorsal and anal fins fringing the body. Seahorses and pipefish, with bodies encased in bony rings, swim by movement of the dorsal and pectoral fins.

BUOYANCY Most fish need to prevent themselves sinking in water. Bony fishes have a swimbladder which is normally filled with gases similar to air; this gives the body 'neutral buoyancy', saving energy in swimming and allowing almost effortless hovering. Changes in buoyancy with depth, as swimbladder volume is altered, are combated by secretion or absorption of gas through parts of the swimbladder wall. In bottom-living fish, the swimbladder is reduced or absent. It is also lacking in the Mackerel, which, swimming permanently in midwater, obtains 'lift' from the extended pectoral fins. The pectorals and the tail fin are also used for this purpose by sharks.

RESPIRATION Fishes obtain dissolved oxygen from water taken into the mouth and passed through gill slits on each side of the front gullet. Between the slits, jointed arches carry red gill filaments through whose thin walls oxygen passes into the blood stream while carbon dioxide and other excretory substances are discharged. A continuous flow of water over the gills is ensured by pumping movements of the floor and sides of the mouth, and of the gill-cover (in bony fish) or gill arch flap (in cartilaginous fish). Skin flaps along the inside of the mouth and gill-cover act as valves. When swimming, water can be passed over the gills if the mouth is kept open – the Mackerel must swim to breathe. The inner openings of the gill slits at the back of the mouth are edged with gill-rakers, long and numerous in fish feeding on plankton, such as Herring and Anchovies, to strain small food organisms from water entering the mouth. In jawless fish, the gills are housed in muscular pouches which act as pumps.

SENSES The most obvious sense organs of fish are the eyes, although these may be small among nocturnal species, such as the Eel, and are vestigial in the Hagfish; most bony fishes have some colour vision but rays

7

and sharks are probably colour-blind. Fish possess an olfactory sac on each side of the snout, opening (usually) by a pair of nostrils; many fish hunt at least partly by scent and a sense of smell may also detect 'alarm substances' released from the damaged skin of another fish. Taste buds are present not only in the mouth but also over the outer surface of the body, especially on the barbels of the Red Mullet and lining the groove of the vibratile first dorsal fin of rocklings. Fishes are also able to register disturbances in surrounding water by means of the lateral-line system – a complex of narrow tubes beneath the skin along the lateral mid-line of the body and around the eyes and jaws. These tubes open at intervals as head pores or, by a short side branch, on each lateral-line scale; inside the canals are tiny sense organs which respond to pressure changes caused by moving predators or prey, or reflections of the fish's own movements from such things as stones or weed. For hearing and balance, fish possess an inner ear although the range of sounds which can be heard varies from species to species. Inside the ears are earstones, sometimes with transparent annual rings useful for estimating age. In the carp family the front part of the swimbladder is connected to the inner ear by a chain of three small bones and serves as a resonating chamber to provide the best sense of hearing among fishes. Sound production is sometimes involved in courtship behaviour and even Cod indicate their territories by grunting.

WATER QUALITY The complex internal body fluids of a fish are separated from the outside water by the semi-permeable membranes of the gill filaments. Under these conditions, water will pass into the body if the concentration of the internal fluids is higher than that of the water bathing the gills, as in a freshwater environment, or leave the body if the surrounding water is more saline, as in the sea. Either way, this harmful effect of 'osmosis' is a problem which fishes must overcome. Thus, freshwater fish get rid of surplus water by producing copious dilute urine, while marine fish drink large quantities of water to make up for loss through the gills; excess salt, unavoidably taken into the body from this water, is eliminated by special cells on the gill surfaces. Only species with adaptable physiology can pass from salt to fresh water, and vice versa. Cartilaginous fishes are nearly all marine and solve the problem in a different way. They raise the concentration of their internal fluids to a level comparable to seawater by retaining urea (a soluble excretory product) within the body. The ammoniacal smell of shark meat is an unpleasant consequence. Apart from salinity, fish are sensitive to other aspects of water condition, such as temperature, oxygen concentration, chemicals liberated by other fish, toxic materials discharged by human industries, and particles in suspension which may harm the gills.

HABITAT AND COLORATION European fishes are found from mountain streams to the ocean depths beyond the continental shelf. Each species is adapted in form and other characteristics for its own habitat. The

HERRING

most obvious adaptation is usually in colour. For example, Herring (above) which inhabits open water has a dark back, like water viewed from above, and silvery sides to match the reflection of light from below by the water surface. Pike and Perch which live among water plants are vertically banded to merge with such surroundings and bottom-living fishes such as gobies have a variegated pattern to resemble the sea-bed. Such patterns depend on the arrangement of special pigment cells in the skin; those can expand or contract under nervous or hormonal influence, so that some fishes – such as flatfish (below) – are able to adjust their coloration to suit the background. For courtship, male fish often display brighter colours and more conspicuous markings, in the dragonets and others on enlarged fins.

FOOD Fishes show a range of feeding habits, from the browsing herbivorous Grey Mullet to carnivorous sharks, and even the parasitism of jawless fishes. Predatory fishes have larger mouths with sharply pointed teeth which may form serrated blades as in the Mako and Blue Shark. In contrast, the omnivorous carps have no jaw teeth but large pharyngeal teeth at the entrance to the gullet which bite upwards against a pad on the underside of the skull. Fish which feed on plankton, such as Herrings and Anchovies, have long gill-rakers to filter out the small organisms from the water entering the mouth. Basking sharks may filter 2,000 tons of seawater an hour if travelling at an average speed of two knots; they shed their gill-rakers yearly during winter hibernation. Jawless fishes use the rasping tongue and horny teeth to scrape into the tissues of other fish for food. To locate their food, fish may use sight, smell, lateral-line sensations and taste and often show daily and seasonal cycles in feeding.

BRILL

REPRODUCTION AND LIFE-HISTORY Fish breed and develop in a wide variety of ways but they all reproduce by means of yolky eggs. In cartilaginous fish, the eggs are large and fertilized internally by the male which has pelvic 'claspers' for this purpose. Some species, such as the Lesser Spotted Dogfish, lay the developing egg within a protective horny case, others are viviparous (ie the eggs develop inside the female and the young are born alive); for example, the young of Blue Sharks are nourished through a yolk-sac placenta while those of the Porbeagle and Mako feed in the uterus by swallowing unfertilized eggs. Bony fishes produce many more but much smaller eggs, forming the hard roe of the Cod and Herring and the caviar of the Sturgeon. In most teleosts the eggs laid by the female are fertilized externally by 'milt' or sperm from an attendant male, sometimes with elaborate courtship behaviour and special coloration. The fertilized eggs of freshwater fish sink onto vegetation or the bottom, while those of many marine teleosts float in the plankton. After hatching the numerous young feed on plankton until they change into adult form. Small fishes, such as gobies and blennies, which live on the sea-bed, often have fewer, relatively larger eggs, guarded usually by the male in a patch or clump under a stone; male sticklebacks construct elaborate nests of weed fragments for the fertilized eggs. Male pipefish and seahorses carry their offspring! Many small fishes reach sexual maturity after the first winter of life and may live no more than a few years. Larger species, such as the Haddock and Plaice, do not mature until they are at least two, sometimes several years old, and may live for ten or twenty years, or even thirty in the Halibut. Fishes breed at times of the year when conditions are most suitable for survival of the young. Around the British Isles, marine species from temperate waters, such as Pilchard and Hake, have long breeding seasons over spring and summer with several broods of eggs, while fish from northern areas such as the Cod, Lumpsuckers and Butterfish spawn once in winter or spring.

MIGRATION All fishes explore their environment to search for food and for mates. In some species, such as the bottom-living Shanny, the extent of this movement is limited; midwater fish, such as Hake, may show daily vertical migrations in relation to changes in light intensity. To spawn, maturing Eels travel from European rivers to the distant Sargasso Sea and Salmon return to breed in European rivers from feeding grounds off Greenland. How migrating fish navigate is still not understood although it seems Salmon remember the particular scent of their home stream.

THE IMPORTANCE OF FISHES Fishes are a valuable source of food and the bulk of European supplies are obtained from the sea. With new techniques of detection, capture and processing, the quantity of fish caught has increased greatly in recent years especially in the 'industrial' fisheries which provide fish-meal for use as animal food and fertilizer. To conserve dwindling stocks, fisheries scientists have suggested certain regulations but international agreement and compliance is difficult to obtain and enforce. Fish-farming, first in fresh water but now in the sea, is developing in importance although, in Britain, it is chiefly limited to salmonids and flatfish. Catching fish is also a popular recreation; again, species must be protected by limiting catches and close seasons, restocking, and by measures to counteract pollution. Apart from angling or eating fish, many kinds can be enjoyed alive in a home aquarium. Given moderately cool conditions and adequate filtration and aeration, some of the small fish mentioned in this book, such as gobies, blennies, minnows and loaches, can be kept successfully while the Three-spined Stickleback will build a nest and breed in captivity.

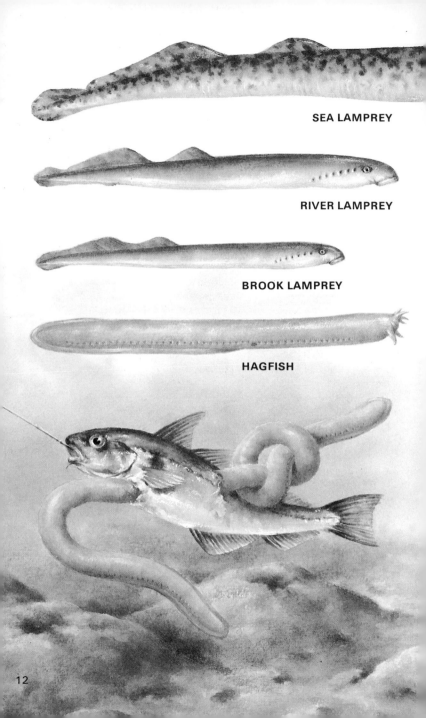

SEA LAMPREY

RIVER LAMPREY

BROOK LAMPREY

HAGFISH

12

LAMPREYS resemble eels but are easily distinguished by a round sucker-like mouth lined with horny teeth (above right), and 7 gill-pores on each side of the head. Often parasitic, the lamprey attaches itself by its characteristic suctorial mouth to live fish and rasps away skin to feed on blood and muscle which is dissolved with special saliva; a round scar is left on the lamprey's temporary host.

SEA LAMPREY (*Petromyzon marinus* 90cm, 2.5kg). A darkly mottled fish with close-set series of teeth radiating from the mouth opening; it lives in the sea until maturity. From December to May, adults ascend rivers to gather on gravel in fast flowing waters where they spawn and die. The large numbers of small spherical eggs, laid in depressions formed by the fish shifting stones by mouth, hatch into blind ammocoete larvae. These move to muddy areas of the stream, and there remain for 3–5½ years, feeding on microscopic organisms and organic particles by means of a filtering apparatus in the gullet similar to that found in sea-squirts. During this period the ammocoete develops into a lamprey of 15–20cm and descends to the sea.

RIVER LAMPREY (*Lampetra fluviatilis* 40–50cm). This lamprey is less mottled on the upper surface and has well-spaced teeth with a plate linking two of these over the mouth opening. Like the Sea Lamprey it migrates into fresh waters usually in September to October and spawns in the following February to June.

BROOK LAMPREY (*Lampetra planeri* 16cm). A smaller fish than the River Lamprey with similar teeth; the dorsal fin not divided into two. It spends its entire life in streams, usually in the shallow upper reaches, and the ammocoete larval stage lasts only 3–5 months. The short-lived adults do not feed before spawning and death in the spring.

HAGFISH (*Myxine glutinosa* 45cm). A marine fish which tunnels in offshore mud. It is characterized by a slit-shaped mouth with short barbels (right) and a side-to-side bite, and a very slippery skin caused by large quantities of mucus from special glands in the back. The species is hermaphrodite and lays clusters of large eggs, each in a horny case. Hagfish eat into dead or dying fish (opposite).

DOGFISHES are small sharks which are common in coastal waters. Like most cartilaginous fishes, they have 5 gill-slits on each side of the head, and a spiracle hole behind each eye; the jaws carry rows of teeth.

LESSER SPOTTED DOGFISH (*Scyliorhinus canicula* 105cm, 4.5kg). A bottom-living fish, on sand or mud, with 2 small dorsal fins over the tail region. It is active at night and feeds on crustaceans, whelks and other invertebrates. Mating occurs in late summer and the eggs are laid mainly from November to July. The embryo is protected by an oblong, trans-lucent, yellowish-fawn egg-case which becomes attached to the sea bed by long curly tendrils; the young hatch after 8–9 months.

SMOOTH HOUND (*Mustelus mustelus* 120cm). A greyish-coloured bottom-living dogfish with a jaw pavement of small rounded teeth; it feeds on crabs, fish or squid. The species is viviparous and produces up to 15 young, each 30cm in length. A similar species the **Stellate Smooth Hound** (*M. asterias* 120cm) has numerous small white spots.

SPURDOG (*Squalus acanthias*, ♂ 90cm, ♀ 120cm, 9.1kg). This slatey-grey fish is easily recognized by the sharp spine in front of each dorsal fin and the absence of an anal fin. Feeding chiefly on fish, it is abundant in temperate seas throughout the world, ranging at all levels in large shoals which move offshore in winter. Spurdogs are ovoviviparous and typically produce 6 embryos, each lying free in the uterus and nourished from its own yolk sac. Gestation can last 2 years, and the young which are eventually born in summer measure 22–33cm.

TOPE (*Galeorhinus galeus* 210cm, 45kg). A larger, more predatory and more shark-like fish with sharp cutting teeth and no spines on the first 2 dorsal fins. Tope are ovoviviparous and move close inshore during sum-mer to give birth to up to 50 or more young (38–40cm long) which can sometimes be caught by angling in sandy shallows.

GREATER SPOTTED DOGFISH (*Scyliorhinus stellaris* 152cm, 9.5kg). A bigger, less common dogfish than the Lesser Spotted with larger brown spots and well separated nostril flaps. It is often found among rocks.

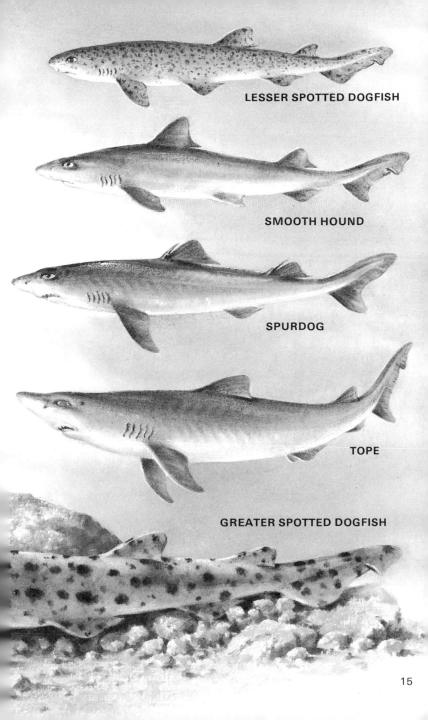

LESSER SPOTTED DOGFISH

SMOOTH HOUND

SPURDOG

TOPE

GREATER SPOTTED DOGFISH

15

THRESHER

SHARKS. Several larger sharks occur in temperate waters, especially during summer. Most are active hunters of mackerel, pilchard, and herring shoals, and, in turn, are caught in a seasonal big-game fishery off the south-west of the British Isles. Their large triangular teeth show character-istic minor differences between species.

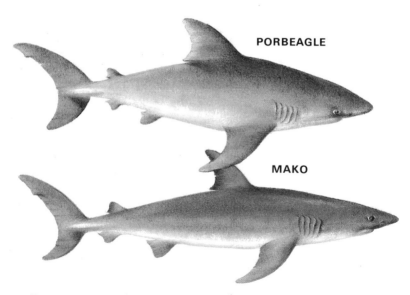

PORBEAGLE

MAKO

THRESHER (*Alopias vulpinus* 600cm, 450kg). Its long tail may be used to concentrate a fish shoal before feeding.

PORBEAGLE (*Lamna nasus* 305cm, 180kg). This shark has teeth with small side cusps, and, on the tail wrist, an extra ridge above and below the main side keel. In summer, 1–4 large pups, up to 60cm long, are born.

With high dorsal fin and tip of tail in the air, the Basking Shark cruises at the surface, its unusually large mouth and gill slits wide open (*right*) to filter plankton. Despite the ominous fins it is harmless to man.

MAKO (*Isurus oxyrinchus* 285cm, 227kg). This species lacks side cusps on the teeth; it is a fast surface fish, and reputed to be dangerous.

BASKING SHARK (*Cetorhinus maximus* 1350cm). A very large but harmless fish which feeds on plankton trapped by long bristle-like gill-rakers fringing the inside of the deep gill slits; the gill-rakers are lost during winter 'hibernation' offshore. In summer these sharks may be visible from land; remains, washed ashore, are often identified as a sea-serpent.

BLUE SHARK (*Prionace glauca* 387cm). Young and spent females occur off the west of Britain; they breed in warmer parts of the Atlantic.

BLUE SHARK

GREENLAND SHARK

HAMMERHEAD SHARK

RABBIT FISH

MONKFISH

18

GREENLAND SHARK (*Somniosus microcephalus* 800cm). A large, rough-skinned, brown or black species with small spineless dorsal fins; it inhabits the cooler North Atlantic, including the northern North Sea, and is the only shark to occur regularly in Arctic seas. Bottom-living in summer, it lives near the surface in winter when it feeds on fish and refuse from sealing or whaling. The Greenland Shark is a lethargic fish and the white parasitic crustaceans attached to its eyes are supposed to attract the fast swimming Arctic Charr on which the shark can feed. The fresh flesh of this shark is poisonous to humans.

COMMON HAMMERHEAD (*Sphyrna zygaena* 408cm, over 400kg). One of the group of sharks named because of their unique head shape which is present from birth. It is formed by a lateral extension of each side of the head and bears the eye on the outer rim. Despite their bizarre appearance, hammerheads are powerful swimmers, sometimes in shoals at the surface; their normal diet is fish but they are known to attack man in warm seas and are related to the ferocious Tiger sharks. The Common Hammerhead is found in the tropics and in summer has been caught around the southern coasts of Britain.

RABBIT FISH (*Chimaera monstrosa* 100cm). This is a bizarre and unmistakable fish with a large head, prominent conical snout, big eyes, conspicuous lateral-line canals over the head and a long tail; male adults have pelvic claspers and a so-called 'head clasper' above the eyes. It is a cartilaginous fish but differs from sharks and rays in having a gill-cover over its gill slits. This species is bottom-living, typically in deep water, but in summer it may move onto offshore parts of the continental shelf where it may be trawled in large numbers. Eggs, in tapering cases, are laid from April to August.

MONKFISH (*Squatina squatina* 183cm, 77kg). A flattened shark which somewhat resembles a true ray except for the large pectoral fins being separate from the head. The species is bottom-living, usually partly buried in sand, and eats mainly flatfish and rays which also inhabit the sea bed. The Monkfish is a warm water shark most frequently seen in northern waters during the summer.

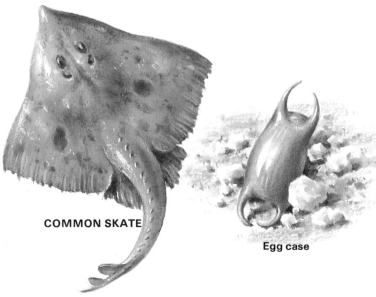

THORNBACK RAY

RAYS AND SKATES (pp. 20–3). These cartilaginous fishes are adapted for life on the sea bed. The many species are sometimes difficult to identify. The snout in rays is blunt but long and pointed in skate. Both have a very flattened body with wide pectoral fins ('wings') fused to the sides of the head, mouth and gill slits on the undersurface of the head, and spiracles on the top behind the eyes. Unlike most fish, they draw in water through these spiracles, and not the mouth, to breathe. Other features include a long, narrow tail with 2 tiny dorsal fins; a reduced tail fin, and a varying array of large thorns and spines on the upper parts of the body and tail. Food is located by scent, the teeth being small but numerous in close-set rows, and the fish swim by wave-like movements of the 'wing' edge. Eggs are laid in horny rectangular cases ('mermaids' purses') on the sea bed and hatch after several months.

COMMON SKATE

Egg case

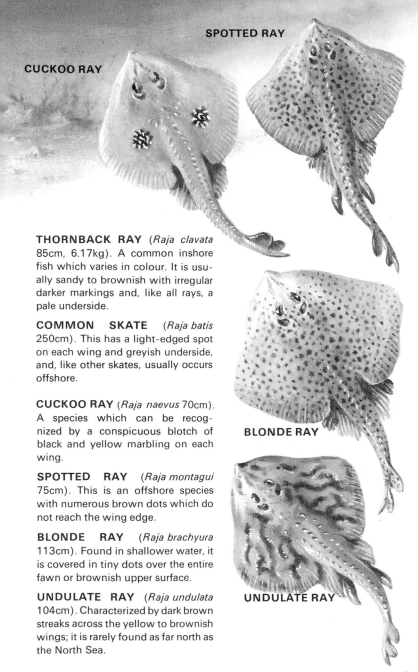

SPOTTED RAY

CUCKOO RAY

BLONDE RAY

UNDULATE RAY

THORNBACK RAY (*Raja clavata* 85cm, 6.17kg). A common inshore fish which varies in colour. It is usually sandy to brownish with irregular darker markings and, like all rays, a pale underside.

COMMON SKATE (*Raja batis* 250cm). This has a light-edged spot on each wing and greyish underside, and, like other skates, usually occurs offshore.

CUCKOO RAY (*Raja naevus* 70cm). A species which can be recognized by a conspicuous blotch of black and yellow marbling on each wing.

SPOTTED RAY (*Raja montagui* 75cm). This is an offshore species with numerous brown dots which do not reach the wing edge.

BLONDE RAY (*Raja brachyura* 113cm). Found in shallower water, it is covered in tiny dots over the entire fawn or brownish upper surface.

UNDULATE RAY (*Raja undulata* 104cm). Characterized by dark brown streaks across the yellow to brownish wings; it is rarely found as far north as the North Sea.

EAGLE RAY (*Myliobatis aquila* 150cm across). A wide body with a clearly formed head, and a very long, whip-like tail with a tiny dorsal fin preceding 1 or 2 serrated spines characterize this species. It feeds on shellfish which are crushed with broad grinding teeth, but also swims in mid water and sometimes leaps at the surface. It is found northwards to the Celtic Sea but rarely strays to the North Sea.

COMMON STINGRAY (*Dasyatis pastinaca* 250cm). This species is kite-shaped, olive to grey-green in colour, and has a long tapering tail armed with usually one long serrated spine with a poison gland at its root. Stingrays are inshore, bottom-dwelling fish, often found partly buried in sandy shallows, and feed on molluscs and fish. They are viviparous and the developing young are nourished by a creamy 'milk' from the wall of the uterus.

COMMON STINGRAY

MARBLED ELECTRIC RAY (*Torpedo marmorata* 60cm). This fish shares the general features of electric rays described below and can be recognized by the 6–8 small skinny flaps which fringe each spiracle.

EYED ELECTRIC RAY (*Torpedo torpedo* 60cm). A species character-ized by 5 large blue spots edged with black on the upper surface and found in temperate seas. Like all electric rays it has a flattened body, very rounded in outline when viewed from above, relatively large dorsal and caudal fins on the tail for swimming, and an oval electric organ in each wing which can generate 25–200 volts for defence or for stunning prey. Not surprisingly a shock from a large ray can temporarily disable an adult human. Electric rays are nocturnal, fish eaters and usually live partly buried on the sea bed; they are viviparous.

EAGLE RAY

MARBLED ELECTRIC RAY

EYED ELECTRIC RAY

23

STURGEON (*Acipenser sturio* 580cm, 408kg). This is the largest bony fish of the north-east Atlantic but it is rarely encountered in any numbers. It is easily identified by the massive body with large shields, an upturned tail and the small protrusible mouth preceded by a row of barbels on the underside of the flattened snout. The sturgeon feeds on small bottom-living invertebrates and fish, using the snout and barbels to locate its prey. Spawning occurs in deep, gravel-bottomed rivers to which the sturgeon migrate in spring, and here the young remain for up to 3 years before descending to the sea. Male sturgeon take 7–9 years to mature, females 8–14, and both may live for over 50 years. A mature female can produce more than 2 million eggs, those of Black Sea species being marketed as caviar.

HERRING (*Clupea harengus*). This well-known silvery fish with one dorsal fin, near the middle of the body above the ventral fins, and a short forked tail fin, is found in the colder North Atlantic. It occurs as 2 main types: Oceanic and Shelf Herring. Oceanic Herrings are found west of the British Isles, grow up to 45cm, spawn in spring and have a life span of over 20 years. In contrast, Shelf Herrings are smaller (rarely over 30cm long), have a shorter life span (under 16 years), spawn in autumn and winter and are found off western Scotland, in the Irish Sea, the North Sea and the Baltic.

All herrings form large shoals, swimming near the sea bed in daylight but moving towards the surface at night to feed on plankton and small fish. In the breeding season, the fish return to the same spawning grounds to

lay small spherical eggs which sink to the bottom. The eggs take from 4 days to 7 weeks to develop, depending on the water temperature, and hatch as tiny larvae (5–9mm long) each carrying a yolk sac; the larvae do not assume adult form until they are about 3–4cm in length.

Herring fisheries have been an important industry in north-western Europe for centuries and the familiar kipper and bloater were traditional methods of preserving seasonal abundance before the development of refrigeration. In the past, drift-net fisheries caught only adults, but modern nets, the use of sonar for locating shoals, and the trawling of immature herrings for fish meal have all contributed to the collapse of North Sea stocks which were once thought to be inexhaustible.

SPRATS

SPRAT (*Sprattus sprattus* 18cm). This species resembles the herring in general appearance but is smaller, becoming mature at 7.5cm, has a sharp belly keel of spiny scales, and pelvic fins which arise slightly in front of the dorsal fin. It is essentially a fish of warm temperate waters, but ranges from the Mediterranean to the Lofotens and into the Baltic. Shoals occur inshore in autumn and winter but migrate to spawn in the open sea during spring and summer when each female may produce several broods of floating planktonic eggs.

TWAITE SHAD (*Alosa fallax* 51cm). This fish shares the characteristics of the Allis Shad but has fewer scales in lateral series (58–70 *v* 70–86) and dark spots along the sides of the body.

ANCHOVY (*Engraulis encrasicholus* 20cm). Easily recognized by its pointed snout and long jaws, this species occurs in summer around the British Isles and into the North Sea but moves south-westwards before winter. It feeds on coastal plankton and breeds from May to August in more northern waters; like the Sprat it is mature after 1 year.

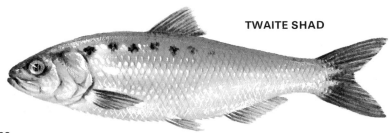

TWAITE SHAD

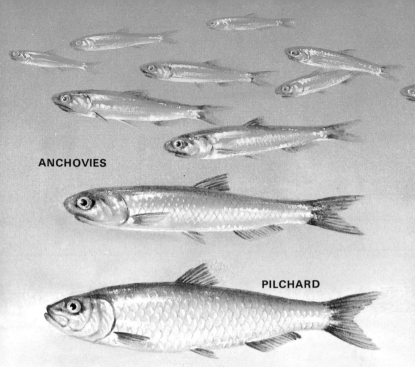

ANCHOVIES

PILCHARD

PILCHARD (*Sardina pilchardus* 28.5cm). Another warm temperate species which can be identified by its ridged gill-cover and the elongated last 2 rays of the anal fin. It is common in the western English Channel during the summer where it breeds from March to October. Sardines are young Pilchards, caught in vast numbers from the Bay of Biscay south to Morocco.

ALLIS SHAD (*Alosa alosa* 76cm). Like many shads it can be distinguished from other herring-like fish by the notch in the middle of the upper jaw. Adult shads ascend rivers to spawn in springtime, laying eggs on the river bottom before returning to the sea at the end of the summer. The young descend to the sea after 1 or 2 years. All species of shad are now uncommon.

ALLIS SHAD

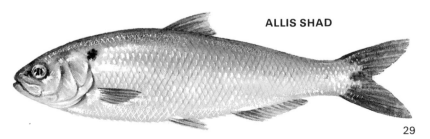

29

PINK SALMON

SALMON (pp. 30–3) are characterized as a family by a small fleshy adipose fin between the main dorsal fin and the tail fin.

ATLANTIC SALMON (*Salmo salar* 153cm, 38.4kg). A much prized fish, valued for sport and for its delicious flavour. It is traditionally fished during the upstream migration to breed: this occurs from spring onwards when the silvery adults ascend rivers, swimming against currents, and sometimes leaping waterfalls, to spawn in shallow streams in early winter. Throughout this period in fresh water, the salmon does not feed and having spawned most adults die as exhausted 'kelts'. The proportion of fish which survive to 'mend' in the sea and become repeat spawners varies with rivers but none has been known to breed more than 4 times. The eggs (6–7mm in diameter) are laid in depressions 'cut' in the river bed by the female, fertilized by the male and then covered with gravel. The breeding male can be recognized by its reddish colour and upturned lower jaw or 'kype'. After some months in the 'redd', the eggs hatch and the young 'alevins' remain among the gravel until the yolk sac is absorbed, usually appearing on the surface by May. The young salmon or 'parr' remain in rivers for 1–4 years, growing to 11–15cm, until, in the spring of the last year, they take on the silvery adult colour and descend to the sea as 'smolts'. There they grow rapidly, often gathering in a major feeding area off south-west Greenland. Salmon may spend 5 years in the sea, though some do return to fresh water to breed after only 1 year. Smaller salmon can be distinguished from Sea Trout by 7–9 anal fin-rays, and 10–13 scales from the adipose fin diagonally down to the lateral line.

♂ in breeding colours

ATLANTIC SALMON

PINK SALMON (*Oncorhynchus gorbuscha* 68cm). This is a Pacific species which has recently appeared in very small numbers off British coasts as a result of Russian attempts to establish it in Siberian rivers. It can be distinguished from the Atlantic Salmon by the lack of dark markings on the body, the larger number of branched rays in the anal fin (12–16 v 7–9) and more lateral-line scales (69–72 v 58–61). Several kinds of Pacific Salmon form the basis of the tinned salmon industry.

RAINBOW TROUT

CHAR

WHITEFISH

GRAYLING

32

BROWN TROUT

BROWN TROUT (50cm, 1–1.5kg) and **Sea Trout** (140cm, 13.5kg) are varieties of *Salmo trutta*. The Brown Trout spends all its life in fresh water, typically in fast clear streams but also in lakes. Silvery Sea Trout occur off European coasts and mature males have a 'kype'; like the Brown Trout, it has more scales (13–16) from adipose fin to lateral line than the Atlantic Salmon. Spawning takes place in fresh water from September to December but the Sea Trout feeds *en route* and does not die after breeding. The trout's breeding behaviour is like that of the Atlantic Salmon and 'parr' can be recognized by 4 or more gill-cover spots, 9–10 bars across the flanks, a red-edged adipose fin and orange-yellow pectoral and ventral fins.

RAINBOW TROUT (*Salmo gairdneri* 114cm, 16.3kg). A North American fish which has been widely introduced as stock for angling and fish farms. It can be distinguished by the dark spots on the tail and the number of branched anal fin-rays (9–12).

CHAR (*Salvelinus alpinus* 80cm). This species is a relict from the last ice age and is found in the deeper lakes of the British Isles, Alps and Scandinavia. Such Char are freshwater fish but in northern Norway they still migrate between sea and river for breeding. Char can be recognized by the reddish underside. The **Brook Trout** (*S. fontinalis* 66cm) is really a Char with a rounded rather than pointed pectoral fin, and dark markings on the dorsal and upper tail fin.

WHITEFISH (*Coregonus* species 40–80cm). This group includes the freshwater **Gwyniad, Powan, Pollan** and **Vendace** found in British lakes; migrant Arctic and Baltic forms include the rare North Sea Houting. All whitefish are silvery coloured, the adult males have whitish tubercles but no kype, and they feed mostly on invertebrates.

GRAYLING (*Thymallus thymallus* 46cm). A freshwater fish with a large dorsal fin which lives in swifter parts of rivers and breeds in the spring.

PIKE (*Esox lucius* 150cm, 35kg). A voracious fish which has powerful jaws armed with strong teeth, and a long torpedo-like body stabilized by rearward dorsal and anal fins. Its characteristic banded coloration enables the Pike to lurk unseen among the reeds and other vegetation and await its prey which can include fish up to half the Pike's own weight, frogs, water-voles and ducklings! From the age of 2–3 years, Pike spawn in February to May, scattering numerous small and sticky eggs (2.5–3mm) over water weeds; a large female can produce half a million eggs. These hatch in 10–15 days, and the tiny larva adheres by its head to weed for 2 weeks until the mouth is fully formed and the body measures about 1.2cm; young Pike begin to eat the fry of other species when 4–8cm in length. Pike live for at least 30 years and are widespread in temperate fresh waters of the Northern Hemisphere, usually in lakes and the slower reaches of rivers. The **Mud Minnow** (*Umbra krameri* 12cm) is a small relative of the Pike which is found in the Danube basin, and sometimes kept in aquaria. It is a hardy fish, living in stagnant pools and feeding on invertebrates. Mud minnows spawn in spring, the relatively small number of eggs being deposited in a hole and guarded by the female.

35

GOLDFISH

CRUCIAN CARP

△

COMMON CARP (*Cyprinus carpio* 100cm, 30kg). A ponderous in-habitant of stagnant waters since Roman times, when this hardy species was introduced from Black Sea rivers for pond culture. It is a deep-bodied fish with large scales, a pair of barbels flanking the small toothless mouth, and a dorsal fin with a long base. It feeds largely on plant material but also small bottom-living invertebrates. Spawning takes place in May and hundreds of thousands of minute eggs (1–1.6mm) are laid. Carp and related fish belong to the most successful group of freshwater fishes which possess pharyngeal teeth at the beginning of the gullet to grind food against a pad on the base of the skull, and a special connection between the inner ear and anterior chamber of the hour-glass shaped swimbladder which greatly improves the ability to hear. Other varieties of carp include **Mirror Carp** characterized by variously developed large scales along the lateral line and back; **Leather Carp** which almost lacks scales entirely; and **Koi Carp** a colourful domestic Japanese variety popular for garden pools.

GOLDFISH (*Carassius auratus* 45cm, 3kg). An Asian relative of the Crucian Carp but with fewer lateral-line scales and a silvery underside; domesticated varieties are well known for their distinctive coloration and fancy fins.

CRUCIAN CARP (*Carassius carassius* 45cm, 3.4kg). This is a similar but smaller species than the Common Carp and lacks mouth barbels. It is found in swampy pools and is very tolerant of pollution and deoxygenation; in extreme cold, it hibernates more or less buried in mud. Spawning takes place in May to June, when 150–300,000 pale reddish eggs are laid.

BREAM (*Abramis brama* 80cm, 9kg). This species has a very deep, laterally compressed body, anal fin with a much longer base than the dorsal fin, and no barbels, though breeding males have white or yellowish tubercles over the head and adjoining body. It is found in large shoals in lakes and slow rivers feeding on weed, dead matter and small invertebrates found on the muddy bottom. During breeding, from May to June, the males defend small territories in marginal weedbeds where spawning takes place with much splashing.

SILVER BREAM (*Blicca bjoernka* 35cm). Found in eastern England this is a much smaller species with red pectoral and pelvic fins tipped with grey.

BREAM

SILVER BREAM

ROACH

RUDD

TENCH

38

ROACH (*Rutilus rutilus* 40cm, 1kg). This species is common in lakes and slower rivers, usually in shoals near weedbeds, feeding on plant material and invertebrates. During spawning from April to June, the male develops white tubercles over the head and upper body and each female lays 5000–10,000 eggs, which stick to plants and hatch in 4–10 days. Stunted Roach are found in overcrowded habitats.

RUDD (*Scardinius erythrophthalmus* 45cm, 1.7kg). A similar species to Roach but it is also found in middle and upper water layers, eating surface insects as well as bottom fauna and plants. The dorsal fin which arises behind the pelvic fin, and the sharp keel between the pelvic and the anal fin provide useful recognition features.

TENCH (*Tinca tinca* 50cm 2kg). This greenish or bronze fish, with small scales and a slimy skin, is able to survive at low levels of oxygen; Tench live at the bottom of stagnant waters and overwinter in the mud. Breeding takes place from May to July and each female lays up to 900,000 small green eggs. The **Golden Tench** is an ornamental variety.

CHUB (*Leuciscus cephalus* 60cm, 4kg). This fish has a thick-set body, relatively large mouth, and dark-edged scales; it lives in rivers, sometimes in shoals near the surface, and feeds on insects. Large Chub are solitary, with individual territories, and more predatory than most carps, eating small fish as well as invertebrates and plants. Chub breed in May to June, and males bear white tubercles.

ORFE or **IDE** (*Leuciscus idus* 60cm, 4kg). This fish inhabits rivers and lakes, moving into sandy or weedy shallows to breed from April to May. Seen in Britain as the golden cultivated form, wild Orfe, found eastwards from Germany, are greyish, with silvery sides, a somewhat stout body, and arched nape.

BARBEL (*Barbus barbus* 102cm, 6kg). Long-bodied, with a prominent snout and ventral mouth flanked by 2 pairs of barbels, this fish swims in shoals by day but disperses at night to feed on bottom invertebrates. Barbel spawn from April to July, sometimes migrating upstream to suitable gravelly shallows. The eggs stick to stones or lodge in crevices to hatch after 10–15 days.

CHUB

ORFE

BARBEL

MINNOW

BLEAK

GUDGEON

DACE

42

MINNOW (*Phoxinus phoxinus* 12.5cm). This is a small species with dark markings along the flanks, a blunt snout and numerous tiny scales in lateral series (85–100). Minnows are common in rivers and lakes, forming midwater shoals in summer but dispersing to deeper water in winter. Spawning takes place from May to mid-July: the male sports a reddish underside and each female lays 200–1000 eggs in clusters on the stream bed. Minnows eat invertebrates and plant material, and are pursued by larger fish, birds and otters; surprisingly their lifespan can exceed 6 years.

BLEAK (*Alburnus alburnus* 20cm). Despite its name, this species is a brilliant silver colour and an essence from the scales is used to line artificial pearls. Bleak are slender, with a superior mouth and an anal fin which has a long base and which arises opposite the rear end of the dorsal fin. Breeding is from April to June; the young are not mature for 2 or 3 years.

GUDGEON (*Gobio gobio* 20cm). An elongate bottom-living fish which has a ventral mouth and paired barbels. It is found typically in faster sandy or gravelly stretches of rivers, and feeds on invertebrates. Spawning takes place from mid-April to late July when about 3000 relatively large (2mm), bluish, sticky eggs are laid.

DACE (*Leuciscus leuciscus* 30cm). A slim, silvery fish with a small pointed head, an inferior mouth, and an anal fin which lies behind the dorsal fin. It feeds on invertebrates and vegetable matter and forms active shoals near the surface of clear, fast-running water. Spawning takes place from February to May, in gravelly stretches of the river. The eggs hatch in about 25 days and young Dace mature quickly, many in the first year.

SPINED LOACH (*Cobitis taenia* 13.5cm). This species of loach has shorter barbels than the Stone Loach and a moveable fork-like spine beneath each eye. It lives in slow or stagnant waters and hides in mud during daylight. Spined Loach are restricted to eastern England but, like Stone Loach, are otherwise found across Eurasia.

STONE LOACH (*Noemacheilus barbatulus* 12.5cm). A small, elongate fish which has 6 barbels around the mouth. It is bottom-living, beneath stones or among weed in streams, and usually nocturnal feeding on bottom invertebrates. Spawning occurs from April to June, when large numbers of dirty white eggs are deposited under stones and guarded by the female; the young hatch at 3mm but grow rapidly.

WEATHER FISH (*Misgurnus fossilis* 35cm). A larger continental loach which is imported for aquaria or garden ponds. The slimy cylindrical body is very long, and the mouth equipped with 10 barbels. Weather Fish lurk in the mud of pools or lakes except when stimulated to activity by falling barometric pressure before a thunderstorm. They can withstand de-oxygenated conditions and swallow air for absorption of oxygen through the gut; in dried-out pools, Weather Fish may survive in mud until autumn reflooding. From April to June, reddish brown eggs (1.5mm in diameter) are laid on water plants and the newly hatched larvae have external gill-filaments.

HORNED POUT (*Ictalurus nebulosus* 45cm, 2kg). A North American catfish which has been introduced to western Europe but not established wild in Britain. It is characterized by 8 long barbels around the mouth and a small adipose fin on the back.

45

WELS or **DANUBIAN CATFISH** (*Silurus glanis*). This is one of the largest freshwater fish reaching a maximum length of 152cm in Europe and 500cm, 330kg in Russia! It is characterized by a large head with 6 barbels, the longest from the upper jaw, a tiny dorsal fin, and, in contrast, a very long-based anal fin which tapers back to join the tail fin. The Wels is usually found in lakes or large rivers where it lurks alone in holes or under tree roots, emerging at night to feed voraciously on fish, frogs, aquatic

birds and mammals, and, according to legend, even a poodle and a little boy! From May to July, numerous pale yellow eggs are spawned over mounds of dead vegetation in swamps or flooded meadows and guarded by the male; the tadpole-like young hatch after about 3 weeks. This species is common in eastern Europe and Russia to the Aral Sea, but less often found in upper tributaries of the Rhine; it has been introduced into parts of southern England.

EEL (*Anguilla anguilla* 142cm). An unmistakable species characterized by a long very thin body, dorsal and anal fins which are continuous around the tail, a lack of pelvic fins, rudimentary scales, and an incredible life history which has only been clarified in the last 60 years. The Eel is very common in European fresh waters where it spends a large part of its life as an immature 'yellow eel', feeding nocturnally on invertebrates and small fish. From September to December, those eels which have become silvery with the onset of sexual maturity descend to the sea undeterred by short overland stages through wet grass. In the sea, the Eels undergo further changes and cease to feed before migrating in deep water for thousands of miles across the Atlantic to the Sargasso Sea where they spawn at depths of 350–450m. Their eggs have never been collected but maturing females have been found to contain as many as 10,000,000. For the next $2\frac{1}{2}$ years, the flattened transparent larvae, known as leptocephali, are carried by the Gulf Stream and the North Atlantic Drift to the north-eastern Atlantic; at the age of 3, the 'elvers' or 'glass eels' ascend rivers, in winter, to grow into yellow eels. Male Eels remain for 7–14 years in fresh waters and reach 24–51cm in length; females stay for 9–19 years before starting their extraordinary migration and grow to a length of 33–100cm. An Eel has lived for 55 years in captivity.

CONGER (*Conger conger* 305cm, 91kg). A marine fish which can be distinguished from the freshwater Eel by the fact that the dorsal fin originates above or just behind the level of the pectoral fins. It is usually found inshore on rocky or coarse ground, though the Conger can occur between tidemarks in large rock pools or under stones on muddy shores where it may be hunted with dogs; Congers feed at night on crabs and fish. They breed in the Atlantic between the Azores and Gibralter, and in the Sargasso Sea, with a leptocephalus larval stage.

△

GARFISH (*Belone bellone* 94cm, over 1kg). An active fish which forms shoals near the sea surface and frequently leaps into the air. Its silvery body is very long, slim and sleek; its head carries long thin jaws which form a 'beak' armed with sharp teeth; the single dorsal and anal fins are set far back near the forked tail fin; and all bones are green. During warmer months, Garfish move inshore to feed on small fish and crustaceans. Large eggs (3–3.5mm), which become attached to weeds by numerous threads, are produced from May to June; the young fish is characterized by the unequal growth of its jaws, the lower being much longer than the upper for a time.

△

SKIPPER (*Scomberesox saurus* 46cm). This species is similar in form and habits to Garfish but has a series of several tiny finlets behind both dorsal and anal fins and lays planktonic eggs with non-adhesive threads. It is a warm-water species and migrates southward by autumn, when cooling may cause fish to be stranded on North Sea coasts.

BLUNT-NOSED FLYING FISH (*Exocoetus obtusirostris* 19.1cm). A subtropical fish which is sometimes seen in the English Channel. Like all flying fishes it possesses enormous pectoral fins which, when extended rigidly, enable it to glide through the air. It lays free-floating planktonic eggs. The **Atlantic Flying Fish** (*Cheilopogon heterurus*, at least 33.5cm) is another species which has been seen in the North Sea in late summer. It uses both its pectoral and pelvic fins and achieves a longer, less erratic flight; the pelvic fins exceed the head in length. The eggs have long
◁ filaments which stick to drifting weed.

▽

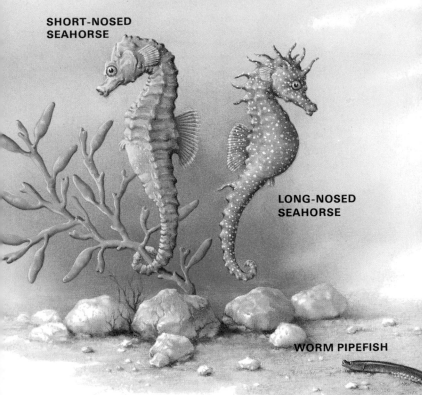

SHORT-NOSED SEAHORSE

LONG-NOSED SEAHORSE

WORM PIPEFISH

SEAHORSES. Unmistakable fish which swim more or less upright, propelled by undulation of the small fins, and with the head bent at an angle to the ridgy, bone-encased body. The prehensile tail is used for clinging to the seaweeds among which seahorses live in shallow water.

LONG-NOSED SEAHORSE (*Hippocampus ramulosus* 15cm) and **SHORT-NOSED SEAHORSE** (*H. hippocampus* 15cm). These are both warm temperate species which may occasionally stray northwards from the Bay of Biscay; they feed on small crustaceans and larval fish. From May to August, male seahorses carry eggs in a large brood sac on the front of the tail base for 4–5 weeks before hatching. During the spiral nuptial swim, with tails entwined, the female may lay as many as 200 eggs into the opening pore at the upper end of the male's sac.

SNAKE PIPEFISH

PIPEFISH. These fish have firm but flexible bodies entirely protected by bony rings; the small head has a tubular snout ending in a tiny mouth used to capture minute animals for food. They swim by wave-like movements of the short dorsal fin but are normally sedentary. Adult males typically possess a brood pouch, formed by folds along the underside of the body, in which developing eggs are carried.

BROAD-NOSED PIPEFISH (*Syngnathus typhle* 30.5cm), **GREATER PIPEFISH** (*S. acus* 46cm) and **LESSER PIPEFISH** (*S. rostellatus* 18cm). The first species rests vertically in sea-grass beds, the second, shown here with a brood pouch, lives in deep water, while the third is common in sandy shallows.

WORM PIPEFISH (*Nerophis lumbriciformis* 18cm) and **STRAIGHT-NOSED PIPEFISH** (*N. ophidion* ♂ 20.5cm, ♀ 30.5cm). Both are inshore species, the former is found among sea-grass and wracks, the latter under stones at low water.

SNAKE PIPEFISH (*Entelurus aequoreus*, ♂ 41cm, ♀ 61cm). Inhabits the open sea and has a vestigial tail fin.

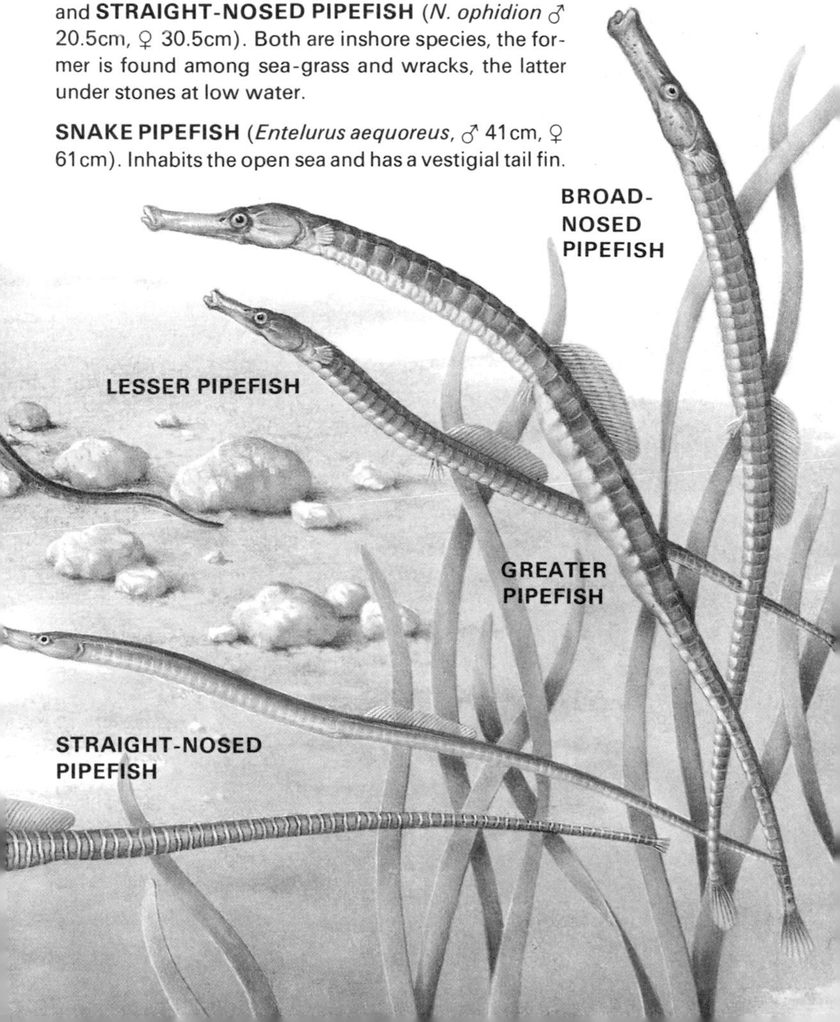

BROAD-NOSED PIPEFISH

LESSER PIPEFISH

GREATER PIPEFISH

STRAIGHT-NOSED PIPEFISH

◁ **COD** (*Gadus morhua* 150cm, 40kg). Like other members of the same family, the Cod has 3 dorsal and 2 anal fins but is distinguished by a white lateral line and a chin barbel usually shorter than the eye diameter. It is an important economic fish of the North Atlantic and inhabits the continental shelf and deeper water to 600m, feeding chiefly on fish and also larger invertebrates. North Sea breeding occurs from February to May on definite spawning grounds; the eggs are small and planktonic and up to 9 million may be spawned by 1 female. Young Cod live on rough nursery grounds until mature at 4–5 years old and 66–76cm. Cod may live for 24 years.

◁ **HADDOCK** (*Melanogrammus aeglefinus* 112cm, 16.8kg). Another commercially valuable fish, it has a very long chin barbel and a dark patch above each pectoral fin. The Haddock's range is similar to Cod's but Haddock are scarcer in the southern North Sea and the Channel. They feed mainly on a variety of bottom-living invertebrates and also on small fish.

△

POLLACK (*Pollachius pollachius* 130cm, 11kg). This species is characterized by a prominent lower jaw without a barbel and a dark lateral line
curved over the pectoral fin. It is restricted to the eastern Atlantic, from the
Mediterranean northward to Iceland and Norway, and frequents rocky
ground often in small shoals. Pollack feed chiefly on fish and prawns, and
breed from January to May.

BIB (*Trisopterus luscus* 41cm, 2.2kg). This is a small coastal species
found in warm temperate waters as far north as the southern North Sea. It
is a deep-bodied fish, with a relatively long chin barbel, coloured reddish-
brown to copper above with dark vertical bands and a spot on the upper
pectoral root; it feeds chiefly on smaller shrimp-like crustaceans. Bib breed
from November to April and the fish is sexually mature after 1 year when it
measures 20–25cm.

▽

△

SAITHE or **COALFISH** (*Pollachius virens* 120cm). This fish, olive to brownish-green in colour, can be distinguished from the Pollack by its pale lateral line, a minute barbel, smaller eyes and less protuberant lower jaw. It is found on both sides of the Atlantic, and is common around northern British coasts although offshore in the English Channel. Spawning takes place from January to May.

WHITING (*Merlangius merlangus* 70cm). This species occurs in the Mediterranean, Black Sea and eastern Atlantic, usually inshore, feeding on fish and crustaceans. It has a prominent snout, a receding lower jaw on which the chin barbel is tiny or even absent, and a small dark spot at the upper end of the pectoral fin root. Whiting have a long spawning season, from January to July, and the young take refuge near the surface beneath large jelly fish until they become bottom-living when 6–6.5cm in length.

▽

LING

HAKE

LING (*Molva molva* 200cm, 40kg). An offshore, mottled-brown fish which has white-edged fins, a darker area at the end of the second dorsal fin and a chin barbel. Spawning takes place from March to July, and a female may produce well over 25 million, perhaps 60 million, eggs. Young Ling may be found nearer to the shore especially on rocky ground.

HAKE (*Merluccius merluccius* 122cm, over 9kg). Unlike Cod, this fish has only 2 dorsal and 1 anal fin and no chin barbel; its mouth is large, black-lined and armed with sharp teeth. Hake are normally found in deep water but move inshore to spawn from April to July, when a large female may produce as many as 2 million planktonic eggs in monthly batches. The species feeds at night on midwater fish and squid and is fished commercially from Morocco to the British Isles.

BURBOT (*Lota lota* 99cm, 24kg). This is the only freshwater species of the cod family; it lives in the cooler parts of North America and Eurasia, including southern England. It is characterized by a barbel on each nostril as well as one on the chin. Burbot feed at night on fish and invertebrates, and breed from December to March, laying batches of eggs in river shallows.

▽

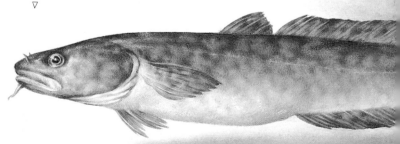

SHORE ROCKLING

FOUR-BEARDED ROCKLING

FIVE-BEARDED
ROCKLING

NORTHERN ROCKLING

LESSER FORKBEARD

THREE-BEARDED ROCKLING

ROCKLINGS. These are bottom-living fish with the first dorsal fin, except for the first ray, sunk into a special dorsal groove lined with taste receptors. All species produce planktonic eggs in spring and summer and pass through a silvery midwater 'mackerel midge' stage.

SHORE ROCKLING (*Gaidropsarus mediterraneus* 25cm) and **THREE-BEARDED ROCKLING** (*G. vulgaris* 53cm). These are the only British species to possess 1 pair of snout barbels. The Shore Rockling is dark red to almost black and found from the shore to about 30m depth; the Three-Bearded Rockling has brownish spots over a pink or reddish body and occurs under stones at low spring tides.

FOUR-BEARDED ROCKLING (*Rhinonemus cimbrius* 41cm). An offshore fish which has 3 snout barbels and white-edged dorsal and anal fins, each with a rear dark blotch.

FIVE-BEARDED ROCKLING (*Ciliata mustela* 28cm) and **NORTHERN ROCKLING** (*G. septentrionalis* 19cm). Both reddish-brown species with 2 pairs of snout barbels, the former is found beneath stones at low water, the latter usually more offshore.

LESSER FORKBEARD (*Raniceps raninus* 30cm). This is a dark brown fish with pale borders to the fins and mouth, and a tiny first dorsal fin. In rock pools, young fish are easily mistaken for real tadpoles; adult fish are solitary inshore and rarely caught.

61

JOHN DORY (*Zeus faber*, ♂ 45cm; ♀ 66cm). This species has a deep, strongly compressed head and body, stout dorsal and anal fin spines and a large black spot on each flank reputedly from St Peter's touch. A coastal species, very widely distributed from the North Sea to South Africa, it feeds on small fish which are carefully stalked and engulfed in its incredibly protrusible mouth. Breeding occurs in summer, and the small planktonic eggs have a greenish-yellow oil globule.

SCAD (*Trachurus trachurus* 40cm). A slim, greenish-silvery fish which possesses separate spiny and soft dorsal fins, a slender tail, a deeply forked tail fin and a row of 70–80 narrow bony plates (each spined) along the side of the body. The species forms large shoals, inshore during the summer, and is common southwards to the tropical Atlantic. It feeds on fish and invertebrates and breeds from July to August.

JOHN DORY

SCAD

RAY'S BREAM (*Brama brama* 70cm). This is a deep-bodied, silvery fish with a rounded head profile and long, scaly dorsal and anal fins. In summer they are found around the British Isles and are often stranded on shores when cold weather reduces sea temperature below 13°C.

COMBER (*Serranus cabrilla* 35cm). A spiny-rayed sea-perch which has several reddish-brown vertical stripes. Solitary but inquisitive, it prefers warm temperate to tropical conditions and is usually restricted to the western English Channel where it frequents inshore rocky ground. Comber spawn from mid-May to August in the Mediterranean; the fish are hermaphrodites so self-fertilization is possible.

RAY'S BREAM

COMBER

ZANDER

RUFFE

BASS

64

PERCH (*Perca fluviatilis* 50cm, 3.5kg). Common in lakes, ponds and the slower reaches of rivers; it can be recognized by its separate dorsal fins, olive-green banding, and red pelvic and anal fins. Small Perch eat invertebrates, larger ones fish. Breeding takes place chiefly in April when females lay up to 300,000 eggs in strands over water plants, twigs or stones.

ZANDER (*Stizostedion lucioperca* 120cm, 12kg). This is a larger, longer Perch-like fish but with no dark spot on the rear of the first dorsal fin and no gill-cover spine. A native to eastern Europe but now introduced into the Fens, Zander are voracious hunters of small fish and their spread is viewed with mixed feelings by British anglers. Spawning occurs from April to June, and both parents guard the eggs in shallow depressions.

RUFFE (*Gymnocephalus cernua* 25cm, 400gm). A freshwater species with notched but continuous dorsal fins; it is widespread across Europe although found only in eastern England. It is bottom living, feeds on invertebrates and spawns in spring.

BASS (*Dicentrarchus labrax* 100cm, 9kg). A silvery, marine fish which is characterized by separate dorsal fins and a serrated rear corner and lower edge to its cheek. It is a warm temperate species, common along south and south-western British coasts; from spring to late autumn, shoals swim up estuaries and may enter fresh waters. Planktonic eggs are laid from March to June.

RED BREAM

BLACK BREAM

MEAGRE

RED BAND-FISH

RED BREAM (*Pagellus bogaraveo* 51cm). Like other sea bream this fish is related to Perch not to freshwater Bream and characterized by a continuous spiny and soft-rayed dorsal fin. This species is reddish or silvery in colour, with a dark blotch above the gill-cover in larger fish, pointed front teeth and numerous small molar-like teeth lying in 2 or 3 rows along the sides of the jaws. Red Bream range northwards from the Channel and Celtic Sea, and lay planktonic eggs offshore in September to October.

BLACK BREAM (*Spondyliosoma cantharus* 51cm). This is another species of sea bream with the characteristic continuous spiny and soft-rayed dorsal fin; its colour varies, but is often silvery with a dark back and vertical bars, and it has single rows of pointed teeth. Black Bream are found offshore to the west of Britain. Eggs are laid on the sea bed during spring and summer and guarded by the male.

MEAGRE (*Argyrosomus regium* 200cm). This is a slender, silvery brown marine fish with a short anal fin; it eats fish and may croak. Large specimens stray to inshore British waters from the south.

RED BAND-FISH (*Cepola rubescens* 70cm). A red or orange offshore species with a body tapering to a threadlike tail. Despite burrowing in mud, Red Band-Fish feed on small crustacea in midwater. During stormy weather, they may be caught on south-western British coasts.

RED MULLET (*Mullus surmuletus* 41cm). A reddish-pink marine fish with yellow side bands and a pair of long, mobile chin barbels which it uses to detect invertebrates on the sea bed. Spawning lasts from May to July and the eggs are planktonic.

RED MULLET

WRASSE are Perch-like inshore fishes chiefly found in warm temperate waters in Europe; they are characterized by prominent lips, strong jaw teeth and pharyngeal molars in the throat.

GOLDSINNY (*Ctenolabrus rupestris* 18cm). This species inhabits reefs near deep water; it is usually brown to reddish with a dark spot on the upper edge of the tail and on the front of the dorsal fin.

GOLDSINNY

CUCKOO WRASSE

ROCK COOK

BALLAN WRASSE

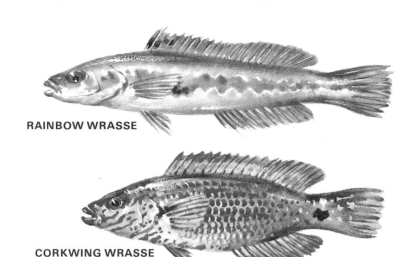

RAINBOW WRASSE

CORKWING WRASSE

CUCKOO WRASSE (*Labrus mixtus* 35cm). This fish is found among rocks in deeper water than Ballan Wrasse. Adult males have a blue-striped head and back, with orange or yellow body and fins; females and young are reddish with 3 dark marks on the rear dorsal fin and adjacent tail fin.

ROCK COOK (*Centrolabrus exoletus* 15cm). This fish resembles the Corkwing but has a light and dark band across the caudal fin; it is found in inshore weed beds.

BALLAN WRASSE (*Labrus bergylta* 51cm). A common British species of wrasse living on rocky ground up to a depth of 10m, feeding on molluscs, barnacles and other sedentary animals. From June to July, the females lay eggs in a nest of fine seaweed, bound by threads of mucus, in a rock crevice.

RAINBOW WRASSE (*Coris julis* 25cm). An occasional colourful visitor to the western Channel, it swims tirelessly near rocks or weeds by day, and buries itself in sand at night.

CORKWING WRASSE (*Crenilabrus melops* 15cm). Common in rock pools and inshore weed beds, its coloration varies but there is usually a smaller dark spot at the base of the caudal fin and the cheek edge is serrated.

GREATER SAND EEL

LESSER SAND EEL

LESSER SAND EEL (*Ammodytes tobianus* 20cm) and **GREATER SAND EEL** (*Hyperoplus lanceolatus* 32cm). These are 2 of the 5 British species of long, slim, silvery fishes with protruding lower jaws known as sand eels. They all swim rapidly in midwater, usually in shoals, but dive into sand when alarmed; they feed on small crustaceans and young fish and are important food for Cod and Mackerel. The Lesser Sand Eel has a protrusible upper jaw and a yellowish colour, and breeds from August to October. The Greater Sand Eel has a non-protrusible upper jaw, a bluish-green back and sides and breeds from April to May.

RETICULATED DRAGONET (*Callionymus reticulatus* 10cm), **SPOTTED DRAGONET** (*C. maculatus* 14cm) and **COMMON DRAGONET** (*C. lyra* 30cm). These are bottom-living fish whose males are brightly coloured with high dorsal fins. The Reticulated Dragonet's second dorsal fin has dark spots interspersed with wavy blue lines and dots; it has 3 cheek spines and is found on sandy ground inshore. The Spotted Dragonet has 4 rows of dark spots across the second dorsal fin and is found in deeper water. The Common Dragonet has 4 rear cheek spines and the male has a yellow second dorsal fin with blue stripes.

LESSER WEEVER (*Trachinus vipera* 14cm) and **GREATER WEEVER** (*T. draco* 41cm). Both fish have a short, black, spiny first dorsal fin and a large gill-cover spine; these spines carry poison glands and inflict painful wounds if the fish is handled carelessly or trodden on by a bare foot. Weevers are found on sandy flats, partly buried by day and feeding at night on small crustaceans. They breed from June to August and the eggs are planktonic.

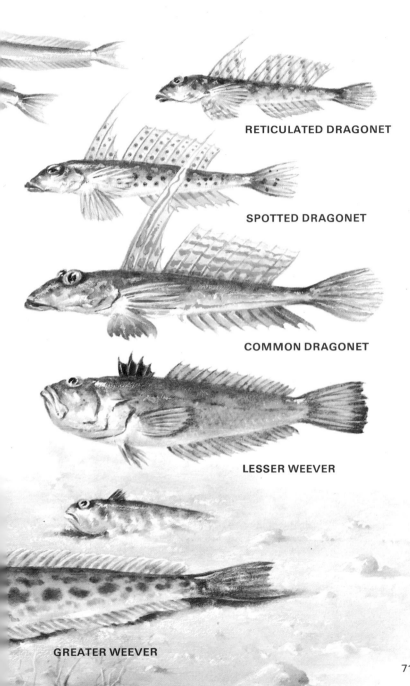

RETICULATED DRAGONET

SPOTTED DRAGONET

COMMON DRAGONET

LESSER WEEVER

GREATER WEEVER

71

TUNNY (*Thunnus thynnus* 245cm). A large oceanic fish which migrates northward around the British Isles to reach the North Sea in summer, it can be distinguished from Mackerel by its size, colour (dark blue with white sides and belly), the corselet of larger scales around the front of the body, and the dorsal fins which are set close together. The species is warmer blooded than most fish and its body temperature may be 10°C above that of the surrounding water; Tunny feed on fish and squid.

MACKEREL (*Scomber scombrus* 46cm). A well-known fish which is found in shoals in temperate Atlantic and Mediterranean waters. It is adapted to a life of continuous swimming with a streamlined head and body, a slender tail and forked caudal fin, and a series of small finlets (behind the second dorsal and anal fins), to reduce turbulence about the propulsive tail. Mackerel are common around the British Isles in summer and autumn, feeding on planktonic crustacea and larval fish, but retire offshore in winter especially into the western Channel. Breeding takes place from spring to September and there are several spawnings of up to half a million tiny planktonic eggs.

LONG-FINNED TUNNY

BONITO

SWORDFISH

SWORDFISH (*Xiphias gladius* 330cm, 136kg in the Atlantic). An oceanic species which may stray to British seas from warmer waters. The characteristic very long, pointed snout, found also in the related Sailfish and Marlin, is flattened in the true Swordfish and the species also lacks pelvic fins. Usually solitary, it feeds on fish and squid, sometimes at great depths; the sword may be used to stun fish when shoals are attacked.

LONG-FINNED TUNNY (*Thunnus alalunga* 93cm). A brownish marine fish which has a blue lateral band and long curved pectoral fins extending back to below the second dorsal fin. The species is common in the Bay of Biscay and occasionally reaches British coasts.

BONITO (*Sarda sarda* 61cm). A small tunny which is steely blue above with silvery sides and undersurface, and a back crossed by oblique dark blue stripes. It is a summer visitor to south-western British waters and is typically seen offshore in dense shoals leaping and feeding on fish near the surface. It spawns from November to January in the Mediterranean and the young grow very rapidly, reaching maturity in 2 years.

GOBIES are typically bottom-living, saltwater fish with pelvic fins fused into a simple ventral sucker. Breeding takes place in spring and summer when the female lays tiny pear-shaped eggs on the undersurface of a stone or shell; these are guarded by the male.

BLACK GOBY (*Gobius niger* 15cm) and **ROCK GOBY** (*G. paganellus* 12cm). Together with the other larger British species described below, these fish mature after 2–3 years and live for up to 11. The Black Goby has a dark blotch on the upper front corner of each dorsal fin; in males the first dorsal fin is very high. The Rock Goby, found under stones on sheltered shores, has a pale-edged first dorsal fin and free upper pectoral rays. The **Giant Goby** (*G. cobitis* 27cm) has side lobes on the front membrane of the pelvic sucker and is found in shore pools in the Western channel.

PAINTED GOBY (*Pomatoschistus pictus* 5.7cm), **COMMON GOBY** (*P. microps* 6.4cm) and **SAND GOBY** (*P. minutus* 9.5cm). These are small species which mature after 1 winter and live no more than 2 years. The Painted and the Sand Gobies are found inshore, the Common Goby in estuaries.

TWO-SPOTTED GOBY (*Gobiusculus flavescens* 6cm). A reddish fish with a large black tail spot; it is found in loose shoals over weed beds. Two other small species, the **Transparent Goby** (*Aphia minuta* 4.6–5.1cm) and the more offshore **Crystal Goby** (*Crystallogobius linearis* 4.7cm) are both midwater fish and live for only one year.

LEOPARD SPOTTED GOBY (*Thorogobius ephippiatus* 13cm). A species with large brick-red spots which inhabits rock crevices of inshore reefs; it was discovered by aqualung divers.

▽

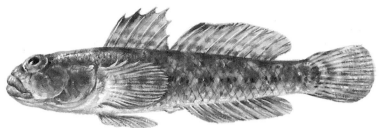

BLACK GOBY

PAINTED GOBY

COMMON GOBY

ROCK GOBY

SAND GOBY

TWO-SPOTTED GOBY

MONTAGU'S BLENNY

BUTTERFISH

SHANNY

Δ

VIVIPAROUS BLENNY (*Zoarces viviparus* 46cm). This fish is found on Scottish coasts and in the North Sea, and is usually intertidal, near brackish water. Mating occurs in August and September, and the embryos are nourished within the mother by an ovarian secretion. Young (10–400, at 3.6–4.6cm) are born in winter.

MONTAGU'S BLENNY (*Coryphoblennius galerita* 8cm). This species lives in high shore-pools on south-western British coasts. It has a triangular flap across the head and blue-white spots, especially in males.

BUTTERFISH or **GUNNEL** (*Pholis gunnellus* 25cm). Characterized by a long flattened body with black spots along the dorsal fin base, this fish occurs under stones on the lower shore, and down to 40m. Breeding of this cold temperate species takes place in January and February and the balls of eggs are guarded by either parent.

SHANNY (*Blennius pholis* 16cm). This fish has a prominent head and tapering body, with narrow anterior pelvic fins. It is common under stones and in pools on rocky shores and its diet includes barnacles and algae. Breeding is from April to August; eggs are laid in crevices and guarded by the male, which becomes dark, with white-edged lips and dorsal fin.

WOLF-FISH (*Anarhichas lupus* 120cm). These are enormous blennies, with large teeth but no pelvic fins. Trawled offshore in the North Sea, Wolf-Fish feed on large crustaceans, sea-urchins, molluscs and fish, crushing these by powerful jaws which can bite through a plank.

▽

THICK-LIPPED MULLET

SAND-SMELT

THICK-LIPPED MULLET (*Crenimugil labrosus* 66cm), **THIN-LIPPED MULLET** (*Liza ramada* 51cm) and **GOLDEN MULLET** (*Liza aurata* 44cm). These are 3 similar species of Grey Mullet found in north-western European waters. Grey Mullet are silvery marine fish with a fairly cylindrical body, short well-separated dorsal fins, and pelvic fins which lie below the ends of the pectoral fins. They have a small mouth with fine teeth for browsing on plants, but also eat invertebrates; they are commonly seen in close shoals over rocks, often in estuaries. The Thick-Lipped Mullet is characterized by a broad upper lip fringed with tiny warts; both the Thin-lipped and the Golden Mullet have a narrow upper lip; the former a short pectoral fin, the latter a much longer one.

THIN-LIPPED MULLET

GOLDEN MULLET

BOYER'S SAND-SMELT

SAND-SMELT (*Atherina presbyter* 15cm). A small shoaling fish, with a broad silvery stripe along the lateral midline, which is found inshore, and in brackish water, during warmer months, spawning in spring and summer. The eggs are attached to seaweed by long filaments and the young form very compact shoals in tide pools or inshore shallows. Sand-Smelt feed on small crustaceans and young fish.

BOYER'S SAND-SMELT (*Atherina mochon* 9cm). A Mediterranean species which has been found in British waters where power stations discharge warm water. It has fewer scales in lateral series than the common species (44–8 v 53–7).

△

REDFISH or **NORWAY HADDOCK** (*Sebastes viviparus* 46cm). A Perch-like marine fish, bright red in colour, with a scaly head and spiny cheek and gill-cover, found offshore in the northern North Sea, feeding on crustaceans and fish. Another species (*S. marinus* 100cm) is of commercial importance. It occurs in deeper water towards and beyond the continental shelf and is characterized by lower cheek spines pointing downwards, not backwards. Both species are viviparous, producing many larvae in late spring or early summer.

GREY GURNARD

GURNARDS are bottom-living saltwater fish with a steep-profiled, heavily armoured head and long, tapering body; the 3 lower pectoral fin-rays are separate and used to raise and move the body above the ground, and possess sensory cells to detect crustaceans and fish for food on the sea bed. Spawning occurs in spring and summer with planktonic eggs and young. Gurnards can grunt by means of the swimbladder. There are several British species including the following:

GREY GURNARD (*Eutrigla gurnardus* 50cm). Typically grey with small white dots, but may be reddish, it has a lateral line of sharp spines and relatively large eyes.

RED GURNARD (*Aspitrigla cuculus* 30cm). A deep red fish with a paler underside and a snout tipped by 3 or 4 spines.

TUB GURNARD (*Trigla lucerna* 61cm). Also red to reddish brown, but it is easily recognized by the bright red pectoral fins, marked blue and green, and a smooth lateral line.

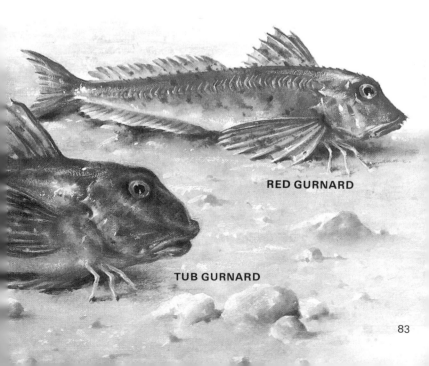

RED GURNARD

TUB GURNARD

SHORT-SPINED SEA-SCORPION

LONG-SPINED SEA-SCORPION

POGGE

BULLHEAD

LUMPSUCKER

84

SHORT-SPINED SEA-SCORPION (*Myoxocephalus scorpius* 30cm). Found around northern and eastern British coasts, it is characterized by gill membranes folded across the throat and often displays white spots on its belly. Spawning takes place from December to March.

LONG-SPINED SEA-SCORPION (*Enophrys bubalis* 17cm). A bottom-living marine species which has a spiny head, large pectoral fins and scaleless body; the gill membrane is fused to the throat and there is a tiny barbel on the corner of the upper jaw. It is common inshore and in sheltered rock pools and preys voraciously on invertebrates and fish. Egg masses are laid in crevices from February to April.

POGGE (*Agonus cataphractus* 15cm). This is a bizarre-looking marine species with a body encased in bony plates; the underside of the head has numerous small barbels. It is more common in winter.

BULLHEAD or **MILLER'S THUMB** (*Cottus gobio* 10cm). A freshwater fish with a smoother, flattened head and low dorsal fins; eggs are laid from March to May beneath stones and guarded by males.

LUMPSUCKER (*Cyclopterus lumpus* ♂ 51cm; ♀ 61cm). A Northern marine species which has a stout body, bony spines, larger plates and a pelvic sucker. From February to May, egg masses are laid inshore and can sometimes be seen at low tide; these are guarded by the males which are blue and red or orange during the breeding season.

COMMON SEA-SNAIL (*Liparis liparis* 12cm) and **MONTAGU'S SEA-SNAIL** (*L. montagui* 6cm). Sea-snails also possess a ventral sucker but are smaller than Lumpsuckers and have surprisingly loose skin. The Common Sea-Snail is found in estuaries in winter and breeds from December to February; Montagu's is more intertidal and is found beneath stones and among seaweed holdfasts; it breeds from May to June.

COMMON SEA-SNAIL

MONTAGU'S SEA-SNAIL

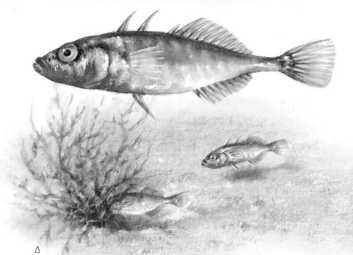

THREE-SPINED STICKLEBACK (*Gasterosteus aculeatus* 6–10cm).
Perhaps the best known freshwater fish, from ditches to rivers and lakes.
This species has 2 large dorsal spines, with a third smaller spine, im-
mediately before the single dorsal fin. The pelvic fins have a strong spine
which can be locked open. There are no scales but bony plates along at
least part of the lateral midline distinguish 2 types of this stickleback – a
freshwater form with merely a few plates at the front, and a larger
estuarine or marine variety, of north-western Europe, where a complete
series of plates to the base of the tail is
expanded there to form lateral keels. The
Three-spined Stickleback feeds on small
invertebrates. Breeding occurs in April
and May, when red-breasted males build
a nest of plant material, glued together
with kidney secretion, and defend the
surrounding area. After a courtship ritual,
spawning takes place and the male
guards and fans the eggs for 1–2 weeks.

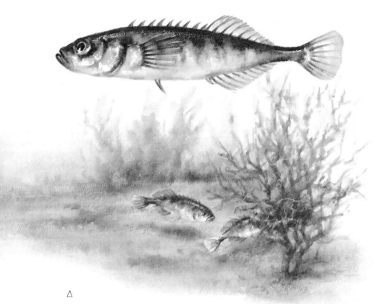

△

TEN-SPINED STICKLEBACK (*Pungitius pungitius* 4–7cm). This species prefers stagnant waters, among weed and mud, though rarely in brackish conditions on British coasts; it has 8–10 small spines before the dorsal fin. Spawning is in April to July; the male is dark, and builds the nest in weed above the bottom.

FIFTEEN-SPINED STICKLEBACK (*Spinachia spinachia* 19cm). This is a much larger, entirely marine, cold-temperate species, with 14–16 small dorsal spines, tiny pelvic fins, and an elongate tail. Fifteen-spined Sticklebacks live inshore, entering estuaries, and are often found in weedy shore pools; they usually eat small crustaceans. For breeding in April to July, the male builds a nest of seaweed fragments in which about 150–200 eggs are laid, hatching about 3 weeks later. Adults die after spawning.

▽

TURBOT

BRILL

FLATFISHES (pp. 89–91) lie on one side of a very compressed body, with both eyes on the pigmented upper side; whether this is the right or left side usually characterizes the species but aberrant 'reversed' examples may be found. All larger species are of commercial importance.

TURBOT (*Scophthalmus maximus* 80–100cm). This is the largest inshore flatfish and swims on its right side; the body is studded with small bony knobs. Adults feed on small fish and spawn in spring and summer, each female producing several million planktonic eggs.

BRILL (*Scophthalmus rhombus* 61cm). Similar to Turbot but it is smaller and has scales.

SOLE

COMMON SOLE (*Solea solea* 51cm) and **SOLENETTE** (*Buglossidium luteum* 13cm). These species are characterized by eyes on the right, a rounded head, a small curved mouth and numerous sensory papillae on the undersurface. They usually inhabit coastal water on sand or mud; Common Soles range from the North Sea to the Mediterranean. The Solenette is characterized by spaced dark rays in the dorsal and anal fins and a tiny pectoral fin.

SCALDFISH (*Arnoglossus laterna* 19cm). This species has eyes on the left side and the upper pelvic fin is much longer-based than that of the blind side.

TOPKNOT (*Zeugopterus punctatus* 25cm). Found in rocky areas, the pelvic and anal fins are joined.
▽

SCALDFISH

SOLENETTE

PLAICE. All the flatfishes of this family swim on the left side like soles but the head is pointed and the mouth terminal.

PLAICE (*Pleuronectes platessa* 51–91cm). This is the most important species economically. It has red or orange spots, a row of blunt bony knobs between the eyes and feeds during the day on bottom-living animals, especially shellfish. The short breeding season during winter or early spring, involves migration to definite spawning areas such as the southern North Sea. Plaice may live at least 20 years.

DAB (*Limanda limanda* 25–38cm). An abundant inshore fish which has a lateral line strongly arched over the pectoral fin.

LEMON SOLE (*Microstomus kitt* 66cm). This fish is smoother and has a smaller mouth than the Dab.

FLOUNDER (*Platichthys flesus* 51cm). Variably coloured on the upper surface, the blind side is always opaque white, and the dorsal and anal fins are flanked by short spines. It lives in coastal waters and the young fish may move into fresh water many miles from the sea. Spawning takes place offshore from February to June.

HALIBUT (*Hippoglossus hippoglossus* 254cm). This species has a thick body with a large head and jaws carrying strong teeth; it can weigh over 300kg and live for at least 35 years. A cold-temperate flatfish, Halibut feed chiefly on fish. Spawning takes place in deep water in late winter or early spring.

HALIBUT

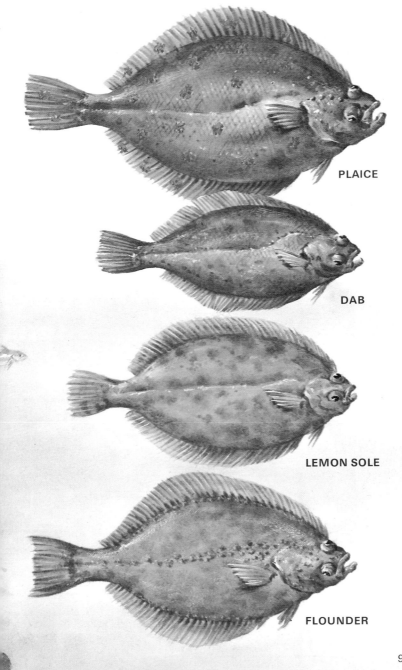

PLAICE

DAB

LEMON SOLE

FLOUNDER

ANGLER FISH

ANGLER FISH (*Lophius piscatorius* 198cm). This fish is a bottom-living predator in coastal and more offshore waters. The enormous mouth is armed with sharp teeth and surmounted by free dorsal fin-rays, the first of which bears a fleshy lure to attract fish or large crustaceans which are then engulfed by a massive snapping reflex. From March to July, millions of eggs are produced in floating gelatinous sheets up to 9m long by over half a metre wide. A more southerly angler (*L. budegassa*) has been found recently around British coasts; this has white pelvic fins and a bilobed lure.

SMALL-HEADED SUCKER

CORNISH SUCKER

CORNISH SUCKER (*Lepadogaster lepadogaster* 6.5cm) and **SMALL-HEADED SUCKER** (*Apletodon microcephalus* 4cm). These small bottom-dwellers, with a complex ventral sucker, are known as clingfish. The Cornish Sucker is red with paired blue spots; it is found under rocks on sheltered shores, often with patches of golden yellow eggs from May to August. The Small-headed Sucker is green or brown with short dorsal and anal fins separate from the caudal fin; it is found at low water of spring tides or in shallows. From May to July, eggs are laid inside the holdfasts of the seaweed *Sacchoriza polyschides* and guarded by the male.

Index of English Names

Index of Scientific Names